The Whispers of a Nameless Love

Mangipudi Anvitha

BookLeaf Publishing

India | USA | UK

Presentation by *BookLeaf Publishing*

Web: www.bookleafpub.com

E-mail: info@bookleafpub.com

ISBN: 9789363301061

First edition 2024

ACKNOWLEDGEMENT

I would like to express my deepest gratitude to my sister, who knew about this book I was trying to write to bring myself back to the writing field and complete my dream of writing. Her unwavering support and encouragement have been invaluable.

A heartfelt thank you to my family and friends, whose experiences and stories of love and longing inspired me to create this collection. Your lives and emotions have been the heart and soul of this book.

Finally, I am deeply grateful to the publishing house for their support and assistance in bringing this book to life. Your belief in my work has made this journey possible.

Thank you to each and every one of you.

Mangipudi Anvitha

PREFACE

Dear Reader,

Have you ever found yourself in a relationship without a name? A bond that exists in the gray areas, somewhere between friendship and love, yet doesn't fully embrace either? This book is born from such an experience, capturing the stormy feelings that arise when you wait for someone who may never fully accept your love.

I've tried to depict the affectionate yet anxious yearning that comes with this nameless relationship—where the connection is deep but undefined, seemingly like friends with benefits but filled with an uncertain love that feels both truthful and deceptive. It's a confusing dance of emotions, where you're constantly torn between waiting and moving on, speaking up and staying silent, all just to remain close to that person.

This collection is inspired by a friend's story, one that resonated deeply with me. Through these pages, I hope to create a space where you can find comfort and relatability in your own experiences. Whatever road you choose to take, know that it's okay. Each decision is shaped by what we feel and go through at that moment, and there should be no regrets for the paths we walk.

May this book be a companion to you, helping you navigate the complexities of love and longing, and remind you that you are not alone in your journey.

With heartfelt sincerity,
Mangipudi Anvitha

Lover's One Night Stand?

Couldn't breathe, I just Couldn't!
Though air surrounds me, free and fair,
I gasp for breath, in deep despair
Wouldn't breathe, I just Wouldn't!

A love so heavy, yet too loose,
Lust blurs lines, confusing the heart,
With an igniting spark and a passionate start.
Well, in the end, who am I to choose?

Navigating through my feelings, I stand unsure,
Seeking the truth through his eyes,
All I see, are a bunch of lies...
And now that I think after all this time, that,
Even the air I couldn't breathe,
Even the air I wouldn't breathe is pure
But am I still?

Meetings and Dates

You call me and say, "Let's go out!"
Before I think it's a proposal,
"It's always so boring with you," you shout.

I wonder all night, without a wink of sleep,
Do you just like to have me at your disposal?

You call me and say, "Let's meet!"
Before I think it's a date,
You bring another woman to make me doubt.

Seeing you giggling and cuddling in the bar
before me,
I question myself: Is this my fate, that I'm not
your mate?

And when you finally say, "Let's go on a date!"
Before I mention my favorite park,
You call out on my weight and debate!

Each time I look forward to our meetings and
dates,
You always, always leave me with a dark
remark!

The Way I See Myself

The way I see...
I don't shine as bright as the stars you admire,
I don't smile as often as your ex used to,
I don't wear the short clothes you prefer,
Still, you stay with me.

The way I see...
I'm not as cool as your favorite anime hero,
I'm not as kind as you are to me,
I'm not as sharp in our discussions,
Still, you talk to me.

The way I see...
I can't be as thin as your magazine models,
I can't follow you at the cost of my career,
I can't perceive every feeling and emotion,
Still, you call out to me.

The way I see...
I fear, you may see the way I see myself.

Lies and Truth?

I asked you to tell me a lie,
You said you slept with her,
I asked you to tell me the truth,
You said you loved me.

I asked you to tell me a lie,
You said you were the one who burnt my career
papers,
I asked you to tell me the truth,
You said you didnt want to leave me.

I asked you to tell me a lie,
You said you deleted my friends' contacts,
I asked you to tell me the truth,
You said you were possessive.

Well, when it comes to lies and truths,
I asked you to tell me a lie,
But I forgot you were full of them to begin with,
I asked you to tell me the truth,
And well, you showed it throughly in your
actions.

Distance and Uncertainty

The weight of not knowing pulls my heart,
leaving me in doubt,
A moment in your eyes when met mine feels
like forever
The very next moment, the distance in your gaze
builds a wall between us all over.

The awkward silence with things we never said,
leaving me to wonder,
Our wordless conversations of emotions and
expressions hang in the air,
And each of your actions, ties a knot I cannot
untie, churning my insides, I swear!

In the dull light of uncertainty, I search for
clarity in your eyes, leaving me confused,
Whilst your lies are the pie on my table of
questions, I hear my own midnight cries,
Your slow pleasure and affection makes me
hush; is it your way to apologize?

Yes, I know that you care, leaving me clueless,
You say your Love and Assurance for our
nameless bond is the key?

However, I know with certainty that all I see is
Distance and Uncertainty!

Before was Simpler

Before, as friends, there was warmth in your
voice, now there's a tone of anger in yours!
Before the lines blurred and hearts became
unsure,
We laughed, cried, held a bond unspoken,
But now, I am one of those, who is broken.

I reminisce about before when I was your
priority,
Now I question my rank, lost in this disparity.
This shift from friends to something more, is it
my fault or yours?
Wasn't it you who lured me in when I was
feeling insecure?

Before, our eyes spoke the bond of friendship,
now our bodies only know how to break it.
If this is the storm we must endure, will you ever
let me quit?
Before was simpler, where friendship knew no
shame,
Now we navigate this chaos, wondering who's
to blame.

Guilt of Loving and Being Loved

As I sacrifice my body and pride, each night a
piece of me fades,
The trust my parents placed in the promises I
made,
Unaware, this is just guilt wrapped in a facade.

A burden I bear, growing myself thin,
Just to stay by your side and suppress my desires
within.
Desperation tears me between my love and kin.

How should I face the tears in their eyes, the
pain of betrayal,
When they see their only child, lost in soul and
body, so frail.
Walking a tightrope between duty and desire,
My soul burns with guilt, in an unending fire.

Why Isn't It Just Me?

I gave you all my pieces, my body, my soul,
Hoping you'd fill the void, make me whole.
Yet in the dance of our nameless bond,
Your touch feels cold, my heart beyond.

Why isn't it only me, I ask, as I ache for the love
you share so freely.

In the silence of the night, I wonder what you're
thinking,
When your gaze searches for her, and mine is
left sinking.
I yearn for a touch, a whisper, a sign,
A voice that says, I'm more than just a moment,
isnt it fine?

Why isn't it only me, I ask, as I ache for the love
you share so freely.

I'm left with shadows and words unsaid,
While you share your affection, so easily spread.
Jealousy or envy, or it's more than just pain,
It's the call of a painful heart that can't explain.

Why isn't it only me, I ask, as I ache for the love
you share so freely.

So tell me, what am I in your list of grand
benefits?
Just another thing, or do our hearts love each
other until one forefeits?
In the midst of your affection, so freely given,
Why isn't it just me, the only reason you are
driven?

Why isn't it only me, I ask, as I ache for the love
you share so freely.

The Regret of Thornful Yesterdays

Why did I ever meet you, when all I feel now is regret?
We had great memories as friends, simple and clear,
Then, with a couple of drinks, everything changed overnight,
The first was a mistake, but what about the second, third, fourth?

Was I really drinking every day, sinking deeper into this?
Was I this pathetic before, or did I lose my way?
Did I forget my God's plans, swallowed by such desires,
Now, my everyday thoughts are filled with regrets and doubts.

I regret meeting you, entangling in this web of emotions,
I regret the memories, now tainted by confusion of our relation,
I regret thinking we could repair this nameless bond,

That you labeled as love, yet feels more like a
trap of a lotus pond.

Each day, I face my own realizations, tough yet
clear,
I regret continuing this, making things
ambiguous,
Only to stay by your side a little longer,
I regret loving you, with every fiber of my
being.

And now I realise, I am the hand that grasps the
thorn,
Believing in the beauty of the Flower,
Only to bleed in vain and remind that each
touch,
Of this love, was never meant to sustain.

Shattered Mirror's Reflection of Reality

Why do I still cling to you, a delusion I can't
shake?
Each effort, each longing, each yearning,
another silent ache.
Accepting the reality, no matter how hard I try,
how much I pry,
There's no point of return, only tears left to dry.

My love is like sending a message to someone
who's blocked me,
No response unless they unblock, no love unless
they set me free.
Once they're done, we're back to square one,
It becomes so hurtful—should I lie and say you
have a son?

Even unborn babies are given love and names,
But our relationship remains nameless after all
this time; am I to blame?
Sweet words from your lips, though I knew they
were fake,
More dangerous than diabetes, a risk I had to
take.

The dream world you showed, a shattered glass
in reality,
Reflecting myself, a fool in stark brutality.
Knowing I was never your one and only, just
one of many,
Handling this truth is painful, regretful, uncanny.

Accepting the reality that I'm just a shadow in
your light,
A nameless bond that fades into the night.
Through my own mirror, I see the fool I've been,
Lost in your promises, a love never seen.

The Vulnerable Me - If We Separate?

With the harsh reality and thought of separation,
I tremble in fear with the void you'll leave,
This reality and my next steps—should I start to
breathe?
Or should I stay, all over again, out of
desperation.

Each day to day, our routines together,
If we break, chaos will cloud my mind,
Each night without you, I might render myself
blind,
Only to find ourselves together, with no reason
left to untether.

If we part, there will be no meetings or dates,
And neither jealousy nor envy exists if you bring
other women,
And no attention or care I'll receive, if I remain
sullen,
And us living together, whose will next replace
my plate?

To run away from you, can I bear the strain?

What becomes of me, without your constant
refrain,
Is there a life beyond this suffering, a peace I
can gain?
Will my heart endure, or succumb to the pain?

My vulnerability, a testament to the love I gave,
In accepting reality, can I find my way?
Embracing my vulnerability, can I face each
day?
And can I face the storm alone, learning to be
brave.

Forgiveness and Break Up?

After countless sleepless nights, I made up my
mind,
I finally broke up with him, I finally did. Did I?
Am I truly free from his lingering shadow?
Will he accept my one-sided decision to part?

Will he stop reaching out, or will the past haunt
me?
Because I am ready to forgive both him and
myself, Am I?
I will forgive him and myself, will I? For our
consensual dance,
I should, as the decisions involved both sides,
two hearts entangled.

Two adults with different paths, trying to stay
closer.
Even parallel lines intersect from a certain angle,
unlike us.
I hope this step of forgiveness and break up,
Is one step closer to the peace I yearn so much.
Is it?

It feels strange that the love I once yearned for
so deeply,

Has vanished, replaced by a yearning for peace
and quiet.
But after all this time, is it truly okay to forgive
him?
The pain I endured, akin to a patient in an
asylum.

I want to forgive you, yes, at least for the parts
Where my heart played along with yours.
But not for the chapters where I was absent,
Not for the wounds you inflicted without my
presence, Isn't it?

Resilience n' Repetition

Days turned into weeks,
Yet the weight of heartache remains.
It's crushing my spirit from the inside,
In the tears you caused, I search for courage,
In the wounds you inflicted,
I tend to seek power.

I distract myself,
Changing my regular shampoo and bedsheets,
To unnamed brands and fabrics.
So that neither the air around me,
Nor I smell or feel like you.

With a smiling face before others,
Like a tree that bends but does not break,
I strive to become resilient and strong,
In the storm's wake,
within my own resolve.

Choosing Hope's Embrace!

Came along my friends, watching me cry,
Stayed through the nights to care.
I began to ascend through their unwavering
faith,
Only to sink even deeper in despair.

"Time heals everything," they say,
"Just forget it ever happened," is all I hear.
If forgetting were that easy, I'd wish to forget,
Not the other girls, but our best moments.

Slowly, their kindness seeped into my soul,
Trying to mend my shattered heart.
Will sealing away my pain make me strong,
Or will facing it head-on make me weep?

Trying to understand my surroundings,
I feel a sense of no belonging.
As if I am the only one enduring,
The pain growing within my wretched heart.

But the love I received from my friends,
Was no less than any mighty mountain.
And as time went on,

I embraced my destiny, with loved ones beside
me.

With hope as my new light,
I watch the dawn waking me to new starts,
And I know for sure, that one day,
I will stand tall with nothing to hide.

Healing: Journey through the Tunnel

In the dim tunnel, I see a glimmer of light,
Each step I take is heavy, yet the world around
me changed,
I notice the vibrant leaves, the rustling trees,
Things I never saw before, make me feel the
warmth of possibility.

My heart, once tethered to sorrow, now I won't
give up.
As I walk towards the light, I feel the pull of the
past,
Trying to reclaim me, a chain of his messages as
a haunting ghost,
Before I would've bent, but now I refuse to wear.

The memories of chores done, not love given,
I realize he misses my presence, not for me,
But for the convenience I provided.
If I step back, the pain will remain, stagnant and
suffocating.

Thankful for friends who remind me of my
strength,
Who guide me towards true healing.

Their voices, a chorus of support,
Drown out the whispers of doubt, telling me to
forge ahead.

Am I truly healing if I let his words pull me back
into the darkness?
My heart debates, but my soul knows the truth.
Even though the past clings to me, I know I
mustn't waver,
Each step is a declaration of my worth, a proof
of the pain.

I know for sure, that healing myself is not a
goal,
Healing is not a destination, not the end,
But a journey I must continue, I must strive,
Despite the shadows and chain that bound till
the end of the tunnel!

Broken Chains: Path to Redemption

I walk in silence, the weight of guilt pressing
down,
Questioning the paths I took, the mistakes I've
made.
Was it my fault, letting him into my world,
Giving him my heart and soul, allowing the hurt
to take root?

In this quiet space, I try to find the courage to
forgive,
Both him and myself, for the roles we played,
the pain I bear.
The chains of the past, were heavy and pulling
me behind,
Now shatter with each breath, with each step
towards my healing.

Redemption whispers softly, a promise of peace,
As I let go of the burdens, the remnants of
sorrow.
No longer defined by any bonds or strings,
I try, reclaiming my identity, my worth found in
my own self.

I set new dreams in motion, goals born from this
journey,
A future untainted by past regrets.
Strength blooms within, nurtured by the pain
overcome,
A testament to the resilience of my spirit.

Peace sterilizes me, as I release the weight of my
impure sins,
The chains that once held me back, now broken,
now gone.
With each step forward, I walk towards the light,
Free from the shadows, filled with hope and
redemption.

Commitment: Pledge I Pursue!

I decided to commit myself, now that I no longer
wear any chains,
Or do I no longer weigh any burden.
I decided to run towards the final path to the
end,
Of that tunnel I see in my dreams.

I started with changing my regular chores,
Then shifted house to house, blocked every little
nose.
I am standing up for myself through the pricky
thorns,
Only to patiently climb and grab my flower of
peace.

I no longer seek validation in the eyes of
another,
I find strength in my reflection, commitment to
my growth.
I stand before the mirror, eyes meeting my own,
A silent vow, a pledge to the person I've become.

I promise to nurture the dreams of my heart,

With unwavering care through the valleys of
past pains,
Each step a proof to my resilience, my vow to
evolve.
I will cherish who I am and commit to oneself.

This is my commitment, to myself, to my future,
To love that is pure, to growth that is endless.
No longer will I settle for less than true respect,
For love that uplifts, for bonds that inspire and
commit.

Final Closure: The Light At the End of the Tunnel!

In the light of closure, I stand, a soul reborn,
The weight of the past lifting, as I step into the
dawn.
For the first time in a while, I see the vibrant
hues of life,
Emotions swirling, a bittersweet cocktail of tears
and smiles.

Years of endless efforts to move on, to brace
myself, to find distractions,
Have led me to this moment of clarity.
The tunnel of despair behind me, I see the light
ahead,
A fresh start beckoning, the end of this painful
chapter.

Meeting you once more, by chance, has proved
me, that I moved on,
I showed you my strength, my freedom that I am
happy.
No longer caged by our nameless bond, I fly
with my own decisions,
Unburdened and free, ending this love.

Experiencing the world anew, every leaf, every breeze, feels different,
Vibrant, alive, even without you.
Uncertain whether to laugh or cry, I wonder realizing,
That I have truly let go, of our bond, of our memories.

You messaged for your convenience, not for love,
And I now see the truth behind your actions, you are still happy.
Thus, I am no longer guilty, no longer burdened by the fear,
Of making your life worse after our parting, I am relieved.

And so our best childhood is in pieces, ashes burning away,
Yet I find solace in the end of this nameless relationship.
This is my closure, my farewell to a painful chapter,
A final goodbye to the shadows of the past.

In this moment, I am free, I am whole, I am ready,
For a future untainted by our past.
With a heart unchained, I embrace the dawn,

And step forward into a world of new
beginnings, and new relationships.

The New Spring

As the painful chapter ends, my new spring
started,
The faith, hard work and the path I chose in the
end,
Really produced fruits for my labor, my friend!
With every dark cloud, vanish, the sky itself
feels sorted.

Hobbies were once a diversion, yet now a
passion I cherish,
Not as memories to hold of past, but on a serious
note.
From video games to gardening, each thing in
the life I wrote,
All came back, leaving my anguish to perish.

Now I speak with a smile, of the past I am asked
about,
No longer a shadow, just a chapter of pain
among many others.
Comfortable in my skin, planting the seeds of
hope all years,
I continue watering by faith, to let my spring
plants grow with no doubt.

A New Relation?

Once there was a time when I hid my past
relation with my parents.
Now that I spoke to them, reflected on my past
actions, and my strength,
Here I am crying my heart out building my new
relation,
With my old parents.

And they understood, which isn't the usual case
every household...

Kindness really does exist, my friends mended
my broken heart, and
Now the soft words from my parents
encouraging my true beliefs,
My past and present decisions, Really did
wonders.
To me and me.

Talking helps, communication breaks
boundaries. And thus as I always say...

There will be hope either from kin, or from
friends, or colleagues,

And if not them, there will be a stranger, who
neither knew us nor our story,
Smiling whole heartedly, ready to accept us for
who we are. And listen,
I will be the stranger. Just like you all were for
me!

Gratitude Beyond Spring

New Life rebuilt, living in the present,
As I close this chapter and continue new
chapters of my life,
I look back with gratitude and hope.

With each poem, there was strength growing
through,
Storms raging within us all, there is that beauty
of healing,
Each of them in their own way, slowly moving
forward.

From making mistakes, bad decisions, regret and
guilt,
To hope, redemption, commitment and closure.
Each of us will reach the end with a new chapter
awaiting.

As they say, if it is not a happy ending, it's not
the end yet,
I thank you all for walking this path with me.
The journey reached it's final destination for me!

May you find your own strength and joy, love
and resilience,

In every step you take, And if life isn't going the
way you wanted!
May you remind yourself of this journey of time
and pace,

Called, "The Whispers of a Nameless Love"...